Windsor: Then & Now

Windsor: Then & Now

Andrew Foot
photographed by Ian Virtue

BIBLIOASIS
Windsor, Ontario

First Edition

Library and Archives Canada Cataloguing in Publication
Title: Windsor : then & now / Andrew Foot ; photographer, Ian Virtue.

Names: Foot, Andrew (Architectural specialist), author. | Virtue, Ian, photographer.

Identifiers: Canadiana 20210286873 | ISBN 9781771964661 (softcover)

Subjects: LCSH: Windsor (Ont.) | LCSH: Windsor (Ont.)—History. | LCSH: Windsor (Ont.)—Pictorial

works. | LCSH: Windsor (Ont.)—History—Pictorial works.

Classification: LCC FC3099.W56 F66 2021 | DDC 971.3/32—dc23

Edited by Sharon Hanna
Copyedited by Allana Amlin
Text and cover designed by Tania Craan
Map designed by Tiffany Munro

Canada Council for the Arts | Conseil des Arts du Canada
ONTARIO ARTS COUNCIL CONSEIL DES ARTS DE L'ONTARIO an Ontario government agency un organisme du gouvernement de l'Ontario
Canadian Heritage | Patrimoine canadien
ONTARIO CREATES | ONTARIO CRÉATIF

Published with the generous assistance of the Canada Council for the Arts, which last year invested $153 million to bring the arts to Canadians throughout the country, and the financial support of the Government of Canada. Biblioasis also acknowledges the support of the Ontario Arts Council (OAC), an agency of the Government of Ontario, which last year funded 1,709 individual artists and 1,078 organizations in 204 communities across Ontario, for a total of $52.1 million, and the contribution of the Government of Ontario through the Ontario Book Publishing Tax Credit and Ontario Creates.

Printed and bound in Canada

PHOTO CREDITS:
Andrew Foot's Collection: 9, 15, 16, 18, 20, 22 (LEFT), 24, 26, 28 (LEFT), 36, 38, 40, 42 (BELOW), 44, 46, 48, 50, 64 (BELOW), 72, 80 (LEFT), 82, 84

Library of Congress: 30

SWODA: 32, 52, 60, 90, 92, 94, 96, 98, 100, 104

The Windsor Project (Ian Virtue Photography): 6

Walter Manzig: 22 (RIGHT)

Windsor Public Library: 54 (ABOVE), 56, 70 (RIGHT), 80 (RIGHT), 88

Windsor Star: 1, 28 (RIGHT), 32, 42 (ABOVE), 48 (LEFT), 52, 54 (BELOW), 58, 64 (ABOVE), 66, 68, 70 (LEFT), 74, 76, 86, 102

CONTENTS

Foreword • 7
by Ian Virtue

Introduction • 9

• • •

CHAPTER 1
Rise of the Border Cities: 1854–1919 • 13

CHAPTER 2
Roaring Twenties & Dirty Thirties: 1920–1939 • 35

CHAPTER 3
Industrial Powerhouse: 1940–1949 • 63

CHAPTER 4
A Very Modern City: 1950–1975 • 79

• • •

A Map of Windsor: Then & Now • 106

Acknowledgements • 108

Biographies • 109

all
are
all
we were

Foreword

by Ian Virtue

The plan was Alaska.

The "last frontier" had always been a dream destination of mine. I'm not sure if it is the many hours spent watching *Brother Bear* as a 10-year-old, or my all-consuming fascination with mountains, but the itch to be up close to some of the highest peaks in the world has pulled me away from Windsor ever since I was old enough book a plane ticket. In 2020, my plan was to spend a week in the Alaskan back country exploring some of the most pristine wilderness in the world, followed by a week hopping from town-to-town in the Kenai Fjords. I bought more memory cards than I could carry, and I was ready to make Alaska the photographic expedition of a lifetime.

Enter COVID-19. With borders closed and nowhere to go, my hometown became the only place I could turn my lens. I found myself photographing cornfields, wineries, and weddings—but what began as a way to make a little extra cash in the middle of a pandemic turned into one of the most fulfilling experiences I've ever had as a photographer.

To be frank, photographing Windsor-Essex County isn't easy. There are no acres of pristine wilderness, cascading waterfalls, or jagged mountain peaks to steal the show in your images. My home is about as flat as the day is long—which is incredible for agriculture, not so great for a landscape photographer. With that flat, unobtrusive geography comes the difficulty of adding depth to your photographs. A good landscape image should always have an engaging foreground, middle ground, and background. The idea is to draw the viewer into the image through each of those points of interest and create a sense of place. A good photograph can give its audience an idea of where they are on this big blue marble we call home. I had spent so much time focusing on finding compelling scenes, I never thought about how I could create them.

In this way, Windsor offers the ultimate challenge because it forces the photographer to not only find those unique locations, but to also seek out the stories behind them. I found myself spending my afternoons poring over old maps, learning about the streets and people that call this place home. What I also discovered, however, is just how much built history we have lost in Windsor-Essex. People have been inhabiting this part of the world for well over 10,000 years and there is very little to show for it. It seems that Windsorites would rather be able to see their car parked in a freshly paved lot than preserve the places that helped to make our community what it is today.

Working on this book has allowed me to really understand how much we have lost. Not only the physical brick and mortar structures that have been torn down, Windsor faces a loss of identity. From trying to photograph the shadow of St. Mary's Academy in what is now a subdivision, to standing in a Food Basics parking lot trying to judge where the castle-like Collegiate Institute used to stand, Windsor is filled with places that once helped to define who we are as a community. Just as I learned from behind the lens, this book will reveal to you the incredible stories hidden in our streets—the backdrops for some of the greatest moments our community has to offer. Places that are worthy of photographing, worthy of knowing. It is a humbling experience, seeing your hometown with the knowledge of who walked before you and stood in the very spot you now stand.

Windsor-Essex finds itself at a critical juncture. A city that can no longer rely on the industries of the past to ensure a prosperous future, we must now look for new opportunities. As we search for these opportunities, the words of Windsor artist Justin Langlois etched into the Imitation Windmill in Olde Sandwich Towne ring truer than ever: "All we are is all we were."

Introduction

More than 20 years ago, I got involved with the history of Windsor almost casually, when I set out to find information on some of the buildings that I saw around the city. In those early days of the internet, I searched online and found no information. A trip to area bookstores yielded a small collection of local history books that helped to fill in some gaps, online auction sites and antique stores would yield old postcards that would raise more questions than answers. That evolved into spending hours at the library combing through microfilm and reading old copies of the newspaper, hunting for details about the buildings that intrigued me. Seeing as the resources were lacking, I decided to do something about it. That is how International Metropolis was born, a website dedicated to the built heritage of our region. I have spent nearly the past two decades sharing these stories online, and creating a community along with it. In the early 2000s, I ended up owning a heritage property, and in 2004 I became a volunteer citizen-at-large member of what was then the Windsor Heritage Committee (today part of the Development & Heritage Standing Committee), and I have been an advocate for Windsor's built heritage ever since. There is a real eagerness to know our history and the past life of our city. *Windsor: Then & Now* is the next step on this journey to discovery—by seeing what once was, we better know ourselves, our city, and where we want to go.

Windsor is an area that has gone boom and bust several times over the years, living and dying with its industrial nature. The city has a rich and proud heritage dating back to the mid-18th century, but when we look around our city streets, it is hard to tell. Why? Windsor is also a city that is constantly changing and renewing itself: chasing an idea of progress it never seems to be able to define. The Windsor of 1900 looked as different to Windsor of 1950 as Windsor of 1950 did to Windsor of the year 2000. Constant change and rebuilding have defined Windsor and the Border Cities.

A European settlement along both shores of the Detroit River stretch back to the founding of Fort Detroit in 1701. A Jesuit mission was established in 1747 on the south side of the river. Despite the Treaty of Paris ending the Revolutionary War in 1783, Detroit remained under British control until the Jay Treaty was signed and the settlement was finally surrendered by the British and turned over to the United States of America in 1796. Those loyal to the Crown were encouraged to move across the river to lands still under British control, and Sandwich officially became a settlement in 1797.

Development has historically occurred along the waterfront: originating in Sandwich with the development of Windsor and Walkerville not far behind. Settler communities grew slowly, primarily growing east and west along the river, and then slowly moving south away from the strait. Even from these early days, transportation has been responsible for the way Windsor grew. Initially, the river was the roadway, with French ribbon farms extending back from the waterfront. The arrival of the streetcar running east and west helped to spur development that filled in the empty fields between Sandwich and Windsor. In the last half of the 20th century, access to the car and roads helped to spur development to the south, east, and to the west. Collectively, the cities of Sandwich, Windsor, Walkerville, Ford City (later East Windsor), Riverside, and Ojibway were known as the Border Cities.

The heart and soul of the city has always been its core. From its earliest days, the city developed along the waterfront, with Ouellette Avenue and Riverside Drive (then Sandwich Street) being the main intersection in town. The ferry dock to Detroit was located at the foot of Ouellette Avenue and a railway station was found along the riverfront at Goyeau Avenue. Many of the finest hotels in the city were found in this part of town as well. Even as the First World War ended, the Border Cities remained small both in population and in development. In 1919, the Border Cities had a combined population of fewer than 50,000 people.

Windsor as we know it today was born of a collection of different municipalities, each with its own identity. Sandwich was the administrative centre and the oldest of the municipalities. Windsor was the big city in the region with most of the services, commerce, transportation, and population. Walkerville was the well-financed and orderly community. Ford City had grown quickly, out of the overwhelming success of the automobile. In 1929, Ford City became the City of East Windsor, changing its name as the Chrysler Corporation opened a new factory at Tecumseh Road East and Drouillard Road. By 1935, many of the communities faced collapsing tax revenues, soaring vacancies and tax defaults, and were nearly bankrupt. Only Walkerville had maintained its financial solvency, avoiding the financial shortfalls of its neighbours. The Province of Ontario stepped in and legislated the amalgamation of Sandwich, Windsor, Walkerville, and East Windsor into a new, larger Windsor that took effect on July 1, 1935. The debt was reorganized and slowly paid off.

The new City of Windsor tackled the debt and moved forward through the Second World War and into the boom of the 1950s. Our collective reliance on manufacturing throughout the entire 20th century shaped Windsor as we know it today. An abundance of well-paying manufacturing jobs for many years provided the region with tremendous buying power, and combined with a relatively low cost of living helped to perpetuate a cycle of new development and suburban expansion. As a result, a cycle of replacing old with new became a part of our lifestyle. Old cars were replaced every few years, houses grew with the families living in them, and buildings around the city were demolished and rebuilt.

Despite all the demolition and new construction, Windsor has a rich history and the development patterns of what were once several different cities and towns all lead to the unique character that can be found here today. Traces of our frontier past can be found in Sandwich, the grand architecture of the Victorian age along Victoria Avenue in downtown Windsor, and in the storied neighbourhoods of Walkerville. Developments from the 1920s are visible everywhere. The great building boom and optimism of the 1950s and 1960s is found in great concentrations in South Windsor.

It wasn't until the demolition of St. Mary's Academy in South Windsor in 1977 that the preservation of historic buildings began to gain traction locally. There seems to be a mindset that progress equals new. The demolition of older buildings and the construction of new ones is always touted as being progressive. However, in the years I have been involved in heritage advocacy, I have noticed a softening and changing of attitudes. The idea of preserving our past has generally been easier to propose, and more eagerly accepted.

Throughout this book you will see pictures of buildings and views from around the city; some recognizable and perhaps many more that are unfamiliar. Numerous buildings have been lost over the years, others are severely altered, and fewer still remain the same. As these photographs reveal, Windsor is a city that is constantly evolving. It is interesting to think about where Windsor will be in another 50 years. How much of Windsor as we know it today will be preserved? Will new developments bring the city into another era of growth? Windsor now, is defined by Windsor then, and taking stock of the city's past means appreciating and understanding the possibilities for our community.

1854–1919

CHAPTER ONE

Rise of the Border Cities

For much of the first half of the 19th century, the Border Region was little more than a sleepy frontier outpost on the southern shore of the Detroit River. The arrival of the Great Western Railway in 1854, making Windsor its terminus, changed all that. Windsor rapidly grew based on that decision, becoming a village in 1854, a town a few years later in 1858, and finally a city in 1892. Along the way, Windsor experienced some growing pains. The early buildings in Windsor were often poorly built, and almost all were made of wood. Sanitation was poor, and no municipal water system existed. Fires were dealt with by a bucket brigade hauling water from the river. In October 1871, the Great Fire of Windsor took out three major blocks in the heart of the city, and more than 100 buildings were destroyed or severely damaged. Only a few of the brick buildings that had been built by that time were left standing. The fire, while destructive, had a few positive repercussions. Ouellette Avenue was widened before being rebuilt with the new construction being done in brick rather than wood and, most importantly, a municipal waterworks and water system was finally approved in 1872.

In 1858, Hiram Walker opened a distillery on lands that he had been acquiring just east of the town of Windsor. The Walker distillery quickly gave birth to the town of Walkerville, with its neighbourhoods of row houses and stately mansions for executives. The town was incorporated in 1890. The Walkers, through the Walkerville Land & Building Co., would build the entire town from houses to churches and schools, while providing services like water, sewers, police, and fire rescue. Walkerville was an early example of a company town.

While Windsor boomed as the main commercial centre of the border region, the oldest community, Sandwich, remained important as the administrative centre of Essex County providing the courts, registry office, and jail. Assumption Church was built in 1845, offering religious services to French-Canadian settlers in the region. The new Essex County Courthouse opened in 1855. Assumption College filled the educational needs of boys and young men upon its founding in 1857. A new Registry Office opened in 1879, and the dawning of the new century also brought a new post office. This proliferation of institutions, with their grand architecture, solidified Sandwich's status as the local centre of government.

The Ford Canada factory opened just east of Walkerville in 1904. By 1913, Ford Canada had grown to employ 1,400 people, and the village of Ford City was incorporated. The community grew like wildfire, with housing surrounding the factory walls. Our Lady of the Rosary Church was built in 1908, with the Ford City Town Hall erected next door in 1914, and Ford City School opened in 1917 on the same stretch of Sandwich Street (today's Riverside Drive).

Windsor and the Border Cities boomed after 1904, with business and people flocking to the region. The Border Cities had come into their own in the early part of the 20th century, and by the end of the First World War had become a major manufacturing centre. The end of the decade saw the population of the Border Cities nearly double from around 24,000 residents in 1911 to just over 44,000 in 1919. While still a relatively small area, the seeds were sown for the explosive growth to follow in the 1920s.

In this chapter we will see photographs and postcard views of the region in those early days, the civic pride that came with grand public buildings, and mighty commercial blocks befitting a growing and important community.

• • •

Designed by Detroit architect Albert H Jordan, this two-storey stone edifice was built as the Essex County Courthouse in 1855. It was constructed out of limestone by Alexander Mackenzie of the Mackenzie Builders of Sarnia, Ontario. That name should sound familiar—Alexander Mackenzie went on to become Canada's second Prime Minister in 1873. This was the fourth court building to occupy the corner of Sandwich and Brock streets. A cell block was added on the southwest wall in 1870.

Several famous trials were held here—most notably for Reverend JL Spracklin, the gun-toting Methodist minister-turned-vigilante who shot barkeep Babe Trumble at a tavern just down the road from the courthouse during Prohibition. In 1943, the last two hangings in Sandwich were held at the courthouse, away from public eyes.

When the new provincial courthouse opened in downtown Windsor in 1963, all of the court functions moved out of the building. It remained in use by Essex County Council until they too moved out in 1974, and the future of the old courthouse became uncertain.

Evelyn McLean, who was the president of the Essex County Historical Society at the time, spearheaded the movement to save the building, founding Friends of the Court. (She would later go on to become Windsor's first heritage planner.) The organization fought to get the Essex County Courthouse on the initial list of seven properties to get a historic designation from the City of Windsor in 1978. The city ended up purchasing the property in 1982, and the building has since become the Mackenzie Hall Cultural Centre—a local hub for theatrical performances, art galleries, and a ballroom for special events.

The **Essex County Courthouse** was an imposing presence on Bedford (today's Sandwich Street) and Brock streets in 1912.

BELOW: Over 100 years later, **Mackenzie Hall Cultural Centre** hosts art and community events instead of trials.

1

A view of the corner of Bedford and Mill streets in historic **Sandwich**, circa 1910.

In 1910, this was Bedford Street, the main thoroughfare of Sandwich—one of the original Border Cities. This postcard shows the new Sandwich Post office on the left-hand side, which had opened its doors on June 1, 1907. The fountain out in front was donated by a prominent former Sandwich resident, William Preston "Press" Leech, who worked for William Randolph Hearst and had risen to be publisher of the *Chicago American*. The fountain was unveiled on August 7, 1909. Sometime after the Second World War, the fountain was removed and its whereabouts was lost to memory. In 1986, a movement was started by the Sandwich Business Improvement Association to locate the original fountain. It was never found, and a replica was built from old photographs in 1990.

The Sandwich Post office closed its doors in 2013. After an extensive renovation of the interior, it reopened as the aptly named Post Café in 2016. The café was shuttered a few years later, and the building is currently in use as an office.

2

Today's **Sandwich Street** no longer has streetcars, but there are still recognizable facades in the region's oldest community.

The **Dougall Avenue School** with its distinctive Flemish gables is seen here in a postcard from 1918.

The Dougall Avenue School was built in the Flemish Renaissance style and opened its doors in 1904. It was designed by the Williams Brothers architects, who are best known in town for their church designs, such as the former Our Lady of the Rosary (now Water's Edge Event Centre) at Riverside Drive and Drouillard Road. When the school was first built, there was some debate if the corner of Dougall Avenue and Elliott Street West was a suitable location, as it was feared that it was too far from downtown to draw students. At its peak, however, the school enrollment was over 700 students. The first principal of the school was DM Eagle, a well-known Public School inspector in Essex County, who now has an elementary school in Tecumseh that bears his name.

3

Today's **Dougall Avenue Public School** is a newer building, but serves the neighbourhood from the same spot.

Today's student population is fewer than 300 at Dougall Public School. At the time of its closure, the building was the oldest local public school. After years of lobbying, funding was granted in 1990 to replace the school. The building was demolished that same year, and the new Dougall Avenue Public School was rebuilt on the same site. The new school opened its doors in 1992. The postcard view above from circa 1918 shows the school with its distinctive Flemish gables. A group of students are visible at the corner of Dougall Avenue and Elliott Street West.

In the early 1900s, **First Presbyterian Church** sat on the northwest corner of Windermere Road at Niagara Street in a quickly growing Walkerville.

In 1907, plans for a Presbyterian church in the Town of Walkerville, to serve as a branch of St Andrew's in downtown Windsor, picked up steam. Scottish Presbyterians were tired of commuting by streetcar every Sunday to neighbouring Windsor. A building committee, lead by Ford of Canada head Gordon McGregor, hired John M Watt to draw up plans for a church to be located at the corner of Windermere Road and Niagara Street in Walkerville. The initial drawings were for a brick structure with a slate roof, supported by steel trusses, with a double entrance at the corner.

A new partnership had formed by the time the plans were approved, and the new firm Watt & Crane oversaw the final design. On May 25, 1908, the cornerstone for the new First Presbyterian Church was laid. The building was built of Detroit stock brick with stone trimming and opened later that year. It was renamed Chalmers United Church in 1933, and closed in June 2001. For a short time, the building was used as a private residence, and today is home to the All Nations Full Gospel Church. The exterior remains largely in its original condition.

Today, this historic church is **All Nations Full Gospel Church**.

4

ABOVE: At the corner Sandwich Street (Riverside Drive) and Ouellette Avenue, **Dominion Bank** was the anchor for Windsor's iconic Norwich Block.

Fast Eddy's, a popular arcade located just west of the bank, was the most popular draw on the Norwich Block after it opened in 1974.

The Dominion Bank opened a branch in Windsor in 1906 in the International Hotel Building on the southwest corner of Riverside Drive West and Ouellette Avenue. The branch proved popular—perhaps by being located on the main corner downtown—and bank officials decided that a more appropriate purpose-built bank building would be required. New York Architects Carrere & Hastings, who had recently opened a Toronto office with Toronto architect Eustace G Bird, drew up plans for the new Windsor bank. Carrere & Hastings were the pre-eminent beaux-arts style architects in America. The new firm employed Bird to oversee the Canadian projects as the architect on the ground, while plans were drawn up in New York City. The building was clad in white Vermont marble on a base of granite from Stanstead, Quebec. The upper floors were designed to house offices and apartments for bank clerks.

The bank, which became Toronto Dominion Bank after the merger in 1933, book-ended what became known as the Norwich Block. The city block became a cultural hub, home to many iconic Windsor haunts such as the wildly popular arcade Fast Eddy's, Eddie Lee's Imperial House, the Spotted Dog Cafe, Elias Deli, and South Shore Books.

Despite public outrage, the entire historic Norwich Block was demolished in 2000 for the Chrysler Canada headquarters. While initial plans boasted a 32-storey skyscraper to replace the city's oldest retail block, the final product was a 14-storey office building constructed in 2002 by Montreal developers, Canderel. As a compromise to the heritage community, the entire facade of Toronto Dominion Bank was salvaged and put into temporary storage at the Lou Romano Water Reclamation Plant pending reuse in an appropriate new development prior to demolition. More than two decades have passed, and the facade remains in storage.

5

The hulking **One Riverside Drive** now dominates Windsor's skyline.

This postcard view, circa 1915, shows the corner of Erie Street and Ouellette Avenue with the original 1890 **Hôtel-Dieu Hospital**.

Hôtel-Dieu Hospital was founded in 1888 by the Religious Hospitallers of St. Joseph, who arrived in Windsor from Montreal. The sisters worked tirelessly to raise funds to secure the six-lot site at Erie Street and Ouellette Avenue, which was on the edge of town in 1888. Windsor's first hospital was built in the Norman style with three turrets, and had 100 beds when it opened in February 1890. Over the years, the hospital grew alongside the community, adding new wings and more beds to match demand.

By the mid-1950s, the older Windsor hospital buildings had begun to show their age. Plans were underway to replace the original wing at Hôtel-Dieu (shown above) as well as the original building of nearby Grace Hospital, which was a century-old residence then being used as an administration wing. A fire that ripped through the old wing at Grace Hospital in 1960 helped to seal the fate of the original wing at Hôtel-Dieu. A new hospital addition opened on the south side of the building in 1962, and the original wing was demolished in 1963.

6

The hospital occupies the same corner, but is now the **Ouellette Campus of Windsor Regional Hospital**.

The sisters of the Religious Hospitallers of St. Joseph worked in every department of the hospital at one time. The last sister retired in 2003, leaving the hospital without a nun on staff for the first time in the hospital's history. The hospital became part of Windsor Regional Hospital in 2013.

The original **Shore Acres Hotel**, at Riverside Drive and Bridge Avenue, is seen here in a 1905 postcard.

The original Shore Acres, a hotel located at Riverside Drive and Bridge Avenue, was built around 1842 by WR Wood, who was the deputy treasurer of the Western District. Oddly, the treasurer ended up in default to the district and left the country. The property was sold and purchased by Col. Arthur Rankin in 1848 and it stayed in the Rankin family until his death in 1893. The hotel then passed to his daughter Phyllis McKee Rankin and her husband Frank Davenport, a well-known American actor. Under her ownership, the house was repaired and renovated with the intention of living in it. This never occurred, and the property was sold to Robert Sturgeon, who renamed it Shore Acres.

There are few hints of the hotels of the past at today's **Ernest Atkinson Park**.

Eventually the hotel was sold to Ben Seigel of Detroit, who demolished the property in 1925 and replaced it with a modern roadhouse, also named Shore Acres. The property originally extended from the river to Tecumseh Road. It was sold off bit by bit until only the parcel from University Avenue to Riverside Drive remained. The property was acquired by the City of Windsor in 1949. In 1953, the city approved the construction of the new Rotary Pool to be built behind the Shore Acres Hotel. The hotel at this time was owned by the city but leased on an annual basis to an independent operator. The pool opened, but the Shore Acres Hotel was demolished at the close of the 1954 swimming season, and the cleared site became Ernest Atkinson Park.

ABOVE: In 1915, the **Labelle Building** on the corner of Ouellette and University was a new addition to downtown's growing business sector.

The bones of the **Labelle Building** were all that was left after a fire ripped through it in 1959.

Dr. James Labelle was a local physician who graduated from medical school in Detroit in 1897 and opened a practice in Windsor two years later. He was appointed coroner for Essex County in 1902, but he also had a penchant for real estate. He lived in a house on the southwest corner of Ouellette and University avenues. As Ouellette Avenue became more desirable as a business location, the doctor had an idea to replace his home with a large business block. He had plans prepared by Windsor architects Crane & Pennington, and his idea came to life in the Labelle Building, which opened for business in 1913. It was a four-storey brick building, with four stores on the ground floor and 23 offices above.

Labelle built a few more properties around town, like the Labelle Terrace townhouse complex which survives today at the corner of Dougall Avenue and Chatham Street. In the first strike of tragedy, James Labelle died in 1923 of a sudden heart attack while behind the wheel of his car in Walkerville. The Labelle building was a very prominent business block downtown, but it fell victim to a massive fire overnight on April 5, 1959. Damage was estimated to be over a million dollars—equivalent to nearly $9 million dollars today. The entire block was consumed, and the remains of the building were quickly demolished. Being a prominent corner in the city's core, the block didn't stay empty long; a replacement building was quickly put up in its place, which still stands today.

A new building opened two years after the fire, which still stands today. There are plans for a new main-floor tenant.

Hiram Walker & Sons Limited was a landmark from its creation in the 1850s. The liquor business created a monopoly of industry down at the riverfront.

In 1856, Hiram Walker, a Massachusetts man and successful Detroit grocer, set his sights across the river and purchased land on the Canadian side, east of Windsor. Hiram Walker & Sons Limited was born on this spot—what began as a flour mill, distillery, and farm would develop into the first Canadian whisky to achieve international fame. The community that grew around the distillery, soon to become Walkerville, was a true company town. People that lived there worked at the liquor operation, and their employer provided housing, streets, running water—even police and fire—at his expense.

In the years to come, Hiram Walker grew into Canada's largest producer of whisky and fine spirits, including its most famous offering: Canadian Club. The company added a ferry service and connected railway lines. It built a lavish head office (designed by Detroit architects Mason & Rice), malt houses, and a grain elevator.

9

The smell of malt still fills Walkerville from **Hiram Walker & Sons Limited**, which is the only major industry that remains on Windsor's riverfront.

Today, Hiram Walker & Sons Limited is the largest "grain to glass" operation in the province, and the largest beverage alcohol distillery in North America. It is part of a Canadian-owned subsidiary of Pernod Ricard SA, and employs more than 150 people. They blend and bottle a variety of brands under the label of Hiram Walker, Corby, and others.

In December 1927, the question of purchasing the Windsor Jockey Club horse racing track to establish a new city park appeared on the ballot to voters. The ballot measure passed, and in 1928 the City of Windsor acquired the site that was then known as "Jockey Club Park." The northeast corner of the park property was sold to the Windsor Board of Education for a new high school, and Kennedy Collegiate Institute, along with Windsor Stadium to the rear, was built on the land.

The *Border Cities Star* proposed in their editorial pages that the Jockey Club Park should be named after Mayor Cecil E Jackson who had fought tirelessly to acquire the property and establish a great park for all residents to enjoy. The movement gained traction with both the Board of Education, Windsor Civic Finance Committee, and finally Windsor City Council passing unanimous resolutions calling on the Board of Parks Commissioners to adopt the name Jackson Park, which they ultimately did.

ABOVE: A postcard view of the **Windsor Jockey Club** in 1915, featuring its grandstand to the left.

Jackson Park, looking southeast from its gates at Ouellette Avenue and Tecumseh Road, 1957. The sunken gardens are visible, as is **Kennedy Collegiate**, in the distance.

Jackson Park was initially known for its sunken gardens, built as a make-work project in the 1930s, including its grand stone entryway at Tecumseh Road and Ouellette Avenue. After the Second World War, a bandshell was built to compliment the old Jockey Club grandstand, and it became a popular space for summer entertainment. In 1957, a massive blaze claimed both the grandstand and bandshell in a devastating loss. Three years later, Dougall and Ouellette avenues were connected via an overpass, splitting the park into two parts.

While the grandstand and bandshell were rebuilt, they did not last—the former being demolished, and the latter languishing without public use. For a time, it was home to the famed Lancaster Bomber, which was removed in 2006 to the airport for restoration. However, its gardens and memorials make Jackson Park a beloved spot in central Windsor.

10

Today, many of the original features remain and **Jackson Park** survives as a gem in the heart of the city.

1920 - 1939

CHAPTER TWO

Roaring Twenties & Dirty Thirties

The 1920s and 1930s were decades of extremes for the city. The Roaring '20s saw a boom here unlike any other period in our city's history. The rise of the automobile and large population growth helped to fuel the boundless opportunity that the 1920s brought to the Border Cities. The skyline of the city in 1929 would have been unrecognizable to someone who was only familiar with Windsor before 1920. Huge building projects brought new skyscrapers and top hotels to downtown. The decade also saw two new important projects: an international bridge and an underwater tunnel linking Windsor and Detroit.

The scope of the region's boom during these years can be hard to visualize today. Between the years of 1919 and 1929 the population grew from just over 44,000 to over 127,000. From the mid-1920s until the start of the Great Depression, the newspapers were filled weekly with announcements of new building projects and new residential districts being opened up, and land speculation was rampant as building lots were being purchased all over the city in newly subdivided and serviced areas.

The boom times of the 1920s quickly vanished as the page turned to the Great Depression of the 1930s. Times were tough: tax defaults on properties rose, unemployment soared, and several border municipalities ended up on the verge of bankruptcy. In the years between 1930 and 1933, more than 13,000 people left the area. The population decline was so steep and rapid that over 12 percent of residences in Windsor became vacant. In response, on July 1, 1935, the Border Cities of Sandwich, Windsor, Walkerville, and East Windsor (formerly Ford City) were amalgamated by the Province of Ontario into the new city of Windsor.

The Depression also brought some positive infrastructure projects to the city to create employment opportunities for citizens. The Dominion Federal Building, Jackson Park, and the Wyandotte-Drouillard underpass were all created during the 1930s. Then, just as the economy started to improve, the end of the decade saw increased global conflict and the return to a world at war. For Windsor, however, the Second World War meant unprecedented demand for the war effort that cranked factories and production back into high gear.

In this chapter we visit the boom years—seeing the optimism that came with new buildings and projects, along with glimpses into the Victorian past. As new blended with old, the Border Cities hurtled forward from boom to bust, and then towards the post-war recovery period and another boom. A selection of photographs in this chapter come from my personal collection and from an amateur photographer's photo album from 1920. The unnamed photographer took a trip around the Great Lakes and one of his stops was Windsor, where he turned his lens on the city. He photographed a rapidly evolving community. Many grand buildings from this period of growth remain all over our city, forming the foundation of the Windsor we know today.

• • •

After the economic jumpstart of the First World War, the Border Cities were well on their way to being an industrial powerhouse. As a result, by 1920, the community was in dire need for a vocational school. Windsor and Walkerville were ready to compete, proposing the erection of the school in their boundaries due to the popularity of the classes in their area schools. Dr FW Merchant, from the provincial Department of Education, recommended that one technical school should be jointly run by the two boards and be built on Erie Street, near the border of Windsor and Walkerville. The nearby location at Giles Street and Parent Avenue was eventually chosen.

Walkerville Technical School, later WD Lowe, on Giles Boulevard in 1927.

The school was built in 1923 and designed by Windsor architects David Cameron and William Ralston. The Windsor-Walkerville Technical School, built in the Tudor Gothic style, opened on August 30 of that same year by the Lieutenant Governor of Ontario, Henry Cockshutt. The school was renamed in 1947 to WD Lowe High School in honour of the first principal who was there from the opening until his passing in 1945. At one time, it was one of the largest schools in the city, with an enrollment peaking at more than 1,600 students in the 1960s.

Over the next three decades, enrollment declined and the school was closed in June 2000. In the years since, the school has been the temporary home of a few schools that were under reconstruction, and since 2011, it has been home to the Giles Campus French Immersion Public School. The future of the building remains uncertain as a new permanent French immersion school, James L Dunn Public School, is due to open in the old International Playing Card Factory a few blocks away in 2022.

In 2021, **Giles Campus French Immersion Public School** calls this historic building home.

11

Imperial Bank of Canada, on the corner of Wyandotte Street and Lincoln Road, in 1934.

12

A historic facade houses a pastry shop and other small retailers in the heart of the **Walkerville neighbourhood** in 2021.

This stately edifice in Walkerville was built in 1927 as the home of the Imperial Bank of Canada. It was the second version of this bank on the corner of Lincoln Avenue and Wyandotte Street East. In the late 1920s, it contained a Loblaws grocery store, the Imperial Bank, and a drugstore on the main floor, with offices for a lawyer, insurance agency, dentist, and the Victorian Order of Nurses on the upper floor. It was designed by Toronto architects Langley & Howland, who designed many bank branches across Ontario for the Imperial Bank. The building today remains largely unchanged, though now it houses cupcakes rather than banknotes, and was designated under the Ontario Heritage Act in 2017.

SW&A **Streetcar Barns** on University Avenue West at Wellington Street in the early 1920s.

Built in 1891 and designed by architect James G McLean, the Sandwich, Windsor & Amherstburg (SW&A) car barns remain today one of the final vestiges of what was once the first electric streetcar system in Canada. The barns were in use even after the SW&A switched to buses in 1939, until the transit company moved to their next home on Kildare Road after the Second World War. The old Cameron Avenue School is visible at the far left in the background. The school was demolished and replaced in 1962, and was renamed Alicia Mason School in honour of its long-time teacher, who served there from 1895 to 1927.

The old barns sit empty in 2021 with the promise of future development.

The car barns site served as an industrial warehouse for many years, and later, was home to the Junction Family Fun Centre. It has been vacant for more than 10 years, with plans to redevelop the buildings on the site into restaurants or entertainment venues coming up short. The recognizable facade is secured on the City of Windsor heritage register and plans are currently in the works for the development of the land north of the car barns into residential housing.

13

TOP: **St. Mary's Academy on Academy** Drive in the early 1930s.

The school was imploded in dramatic fashion in 1977.

St. Mary's Academy was established in 1856 by the Order of the Sisters of the Holy Names of Jesus and Mary as a private Catholic girls' school—the equivalent to Assumption College for boys in Sandwich. The school was originally located on a prime spot on Ouellette Avenue at Park Street in downtown Windsor. By the 1920s, however, the economy was booming and properties in the city's core were highly desirable. The promoters of the Windsor-Detroit tunnel saw the large site as the perfect location for the Windsor terminal of the tunnel linking downtown Windsor to downtown Detroit. The sisters fielded multiple offers for the coveted property until an agreement was eventually reached to sell the downtown location to the Detroit-Windsor Tunnel Corporation. Today, you'll find the Canadian Tunnel Plaza at this location.

A large 23-acre (nine-hectare) site in the newly developing area of South Windsor was donated by Leo Page of Healy, Page, Chappus Ltd., large land holders and developers, while Montreal architects Viau & Venne were commissioned to design the imposing Gothic style school in 1928. The school opened its doors in 1929 and was immediately a South Windsor fixture.

The **Gates of St. Mary** is now an established neighbourhood in South Windsor. The developers built these small, brick pillars to hint towards the past school as a way to appease the public after demolishing the original gates.

By 1966, enrollment had declined and as a result, the school pivoted from accepting boarding students to becoming strictly a day school. The dormitories were converted into classrooms and laboratories. In September 1969, the sisters announced that the private school would close its doors in June 1971. Enrollment was down to 472 students when the closure was announced, rising maintenance costs and changing needs for educational buildings were given as the main reasons for the closure. When St. Mary's closed in 1971, Assumption College Catholic High School became co-ed and the remaining students were transferred there. Many ideas were floated for the reuse of the building, such as a seniors' residence or the new home of the Art Gallery of Windsor—even the reuse of the building as a school. No plans ever materialized, and after being on the market for five years, the property was sold to a developer. Despite widespread opposition and outcry from the public, the building was imploded on April 29, 1977, by Controlled Demolition Inc. The site was cleared and replaced with a subdivision, The Gates of St. Mary, as a nod to its predecessor.

The demolition of St. Mary's Academy was considered by many to be the catalyst in the city to place a value on heritage properties, leading to buildings such as Mackenzie Hall in Sandwich ultimately being preserved once their official uses had ended.

A vacationing photographer snapped this image of **Windsor Collegiate Institute**, on the corner of Elliot Street and Goyeau Avenue, in 1920 during his travels around the Great Lakes.

15

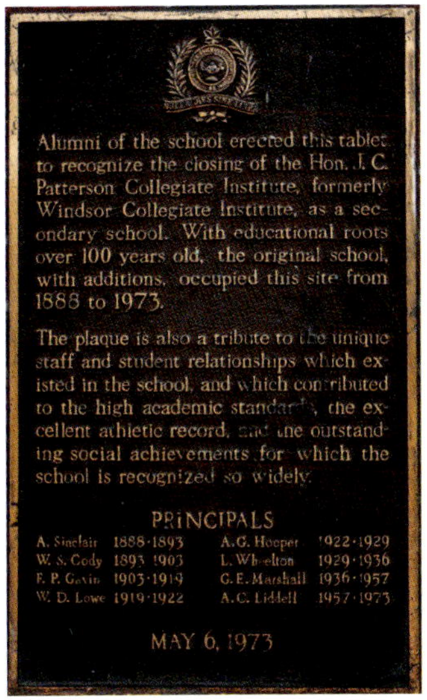

The former community fixture is the current location of a Food Basics grocery store.

This permanent monument and time capsule was installed in 2019 in the corner of the store parking lot.

Windsor Collegiate Institute—the area's first secondary school—was designed by local architect James G McLean, who also designed the SW&A streetcar barns. The building featured a grand turret and tower when it opened in 1888. A large addition, known as the "annex," was added to the rear of the school in 1915, designed by JC Pennington.

In 1930, the school was renamed JC Patterson Collegiate Institute. Patterson was a member of Parliament and held prominent cabinet positions in the governments of Sir James Abbott, Sir John Thompson, and Mackenzie Bowell. From 1895 to 1900, he served as Lieutenant Governor of Manitoba, eventually retiring from public life in Ottawa, where he died in 1929. Patterson originally owned the land that was donated to build the school.

Dwindling enrollment combined with costly repairs to Windsor's oldest school building prompted the closure of Patterson in 1973. For a short time after it closed, the building housed some of St. Clair College's adult training programs, but despite multiple proposals for reuse, nothing materialized and the building was demolished in 1979. The site today is home to a grocery store and parking lot.

Wyandotte Street, looking east from Ouellette Avenue, in 1920.

A century ago, this stretch of Wyandotte Street, running east from Ouellette Avenue, was largely residential. If you look closely, the streetcar tracks are visible in the middle of the bricked road. The building on the north side was built in 1913 as the Independent Order of Odd Fellows (IOOF) Hall, and it was designed by the Windsor architect team of Crane & Pennington. While the partnership was in Windsor, between 1911 and 1914, they were extremely busy. When they split off, C Howard Crane returned to Detroit where he designed the majority of the large downtown Detroit theatre houses, and JC Pennington continued working in Windsor until his death in 1963. The Odd Fellows sold the hall in 1944 to the United Auto Workers (UAW), who made it the home of Local 200. UAW Local 200 remained in the building until 1966 when they built a new hall on Turner Road in unison with Local 444. The old building was demolished shortly after. The site today is home to a parking garage.

One hundred years later, **Wyandotte Street** is virtually unrecognizable.

TOP LEFT: **Windsor's City Hall** sat in the heart of the downtown core in the 1920s.

TOP RIGHT: This modernist **City Hall** replaced the old Central School building in 1958.

Originally built in 1865 as the Windsor Central School by Detroit architect Albert H Jordan, the building served as a schoolhouse until it was ordered closed by the Fire Department Chief Clarence DeFields in 1887. The city struck a deal with the school board and purchased the Windsor Central School in 1903. Following work to convert the building into municipal offices, it re-opened as Windsor's second city hall in 1904. The stately building was surrounded by a treed park—a foreshadowing of City Hall Square in the decades to come.

By the 1920s, talk had already started about the need to replace an aging City Hall with something more suitable. As the building ran out of space, an annex was built. In 1956, it was decided to finally build a new City Hall. The old Central School was demolished and the new in-vogue City Hall was built on the same site. The new site was modernist, rejecting glass walls and opting for striking royal-blue porcelain enamel and limestone on the facade. Designed by Sheppard, Masson, and Trace, the building was heralded by the *Windsor Star* as an "imposing piece of architecture in the 20th century motif, befitting this great Canadian industrial metropolis."

What was new quickly became old once again. Today's city hall—the third in that same spot—opened its doors in 2018. As opened to the grandiose character of its predecessors, this building is open concept with natural light—an architectural decision meant to reflect the city's agenda to provide for customer service and transparency.

On the same location, today's **City Hall** opened its doors in 2018.

Windsor's main post office sat at the corner of Pitt Street and Ouellette Avenue in 1920.

The old post office was built in 1879 and designed by Thomas Scott, who was the chief architect for the Department of Public Works for the Government of Canada. In 1906, a new fountain was erected in front of the post office as a memorial to the soldiers who fell in the Boer War in South Africa. The fountain at the entrance was designed by architect John Scott of Detroit, and the large bronze panel on the front of the fountain was done by Canadian sculptor Walter Allward. Allward would go on to design the iconic First World War Vimy Ridge memorial in France.

By the early 1900s, there was talk of replacing the post office with something more suitable for a growing community. During the Great Depression, when public work projects were popular as a way to create employment, a new federal building was planned for the block where the old post office stood. It was demolished in 1932. The fountain in front of the post office was spared and relocated to Jackson Park, where it sits today in need of restoration.

The Dominion Public Building opened in 1934, a towering six-storeys spanning a full city block. It was designed by a team of local architects including George Masson, Hugh P Sheppard, John Trace, and Guy Buller Colthurst as a modern take on the beaux-arts style with striking limestone exterior walls and intricate masonry details. It was intended as a hub for federal services—a one-stop shop for post office, accounting, and customs.

18

A downtown landmark, the **Paul Martin Building** has been restored in recent years, purchased by the city, and is ready to serve the public.

In 1994, it was renamed the Paul Martin Building, in honour of hometown luminary Paul Martin Sr, the prominent Canadian politician and diplomat. In a historic move, the government vacated the building in 2016, removing a downtown post office which had served the community since the 1800s. The Paul Martin Building was in limbo, needing exterior repairs and a tenant. Recognizing its historic value, the government slowly fixed the facade, and in 2019, the City of Windsor managed to secure the Paul Martin Building for one dollar. It currently serves as a temporary home for the Windsor Public Library.

TOP LEFT: **Devonshire Race Track** was one of three horse racing tracks in the Border Cities in the 1920s.

Race day at Devonshire, postmarked 1928.

Thoroughbred horse racing was made illegal in Michigan prior to the First World War, leaving gamblers looking elsewhere to get their fix. As has often been the case throughout our history, Windsor stepped up to fill that void and offered our neighbours in Michigan a place to get what they couldn't get at home. At the peak of thoroughbred racing in Windsor, the city boasted three horse racing tracks: The Windsor Jockey Club, which is today Jackson Park and Kennedy Collegiate; Kenilworth Race Track, today a housing subdivision; and Devonshire Race Track, today Devonshire Mall.

When it was built, Devonshire Race Track was located just over three kilometres outside of city limits on today's Howard Avenue. It branded itself as a "mecca for Canadian and American racing devotees" and advertised its fine clubhouse and grandstand that featured stone construction.

19

Devonshire Mall opened its doors in 1970, sounding the death knell for many local retailers in the downtown core.

All good things come to an end and eventually Windsor's monopoly on racing came to an end in 1934 when the State of Michigan legalized horse racing again. The Devonshire Race Track saw its last race run on July 10, 1936. The grandstand was destroyed by fire in 1939. From there, its history is less clear—it served as a home for the Windsor Riding Club and even for the racing of greyhound dogs.

By the late 1960s, the site was surrounded by the growing suburbia of South Windsor and the 65-acre property was chosen as the place for Windsor's first indoor shopping centre. A nod to its predecessor, Devonshire Mall opened to frenzied crowds on August 12, 1970.

TOP RIGHT: The **Drouillard-Wyandotte** subway was a make-work project for destitute workers in Depression-era East Windsor.

A blockade of cars filled **Drouillard Road**, as seen here looking north towards the Detroit River from the subway intersection, during the famous Ford Strike of 1945.

In the late 1920s, Wyandotte Street ended at Walker Road and east of Drouillard Road, it was known as Ottawa Street. While we commonly think of a subway as being a mass transportation system, this subway refers to the road and underpass under the railway tracks. The underpass was originally envisioned as a north-south subway under the Canadian National Railway tracks. The plan grew to become a double subway, featuring an east-west Wyandotte Street extension, when the town of Walkerville decided to move ahead with a second subway under the Pere Marquette Railway tracks a bit to the west. Both the East Windsor and Walkerville subways became relief projects putting many local residents to work during the Great Depression. Workers were compensated with meal and coal vouchers.

It is amazing how quickly the project came together. The Dominion Railway Board authorized the construction of the North-South Drouillard Road subway in December 1929, with permission for the Wyandotte Street half approved in July 1930. At a special meeting of the East Windsor City Council, city engineer HW Patterson was authorized to prepare plans and specifications and to call tenders for the subway on August 22, 1930. The tenders were awarded on September 9, 1930, and the subway opened to traffic in October 1931. Today, the subway is more commonly known as the Drouillard Road underpass and is considered the entryway to old Ford City (East Windsor)—a neighbourhood that embraces its automotive heritage.

20

LEFT: The underpass marks one of the more unique—and accident-prone—intersections in the city.

TOP LEFT: A Model T sign marks the entrance to old Ford City.

1000 Drouillard Road was home to the Crown Cafe, at **Drouillard Road** and **Charles (Whelpton) Street**, in the late 1920s.

A funky taco joint with a bright neon sign, the Grand Cantina, was one of the first of several businesses to open up on **Drouillard Road** in recent years.

In 1904, the Ford Motor Company of Canada factory was established along the Detroit River. Over time, the Ford operations grew and the main street of Ford City, Drouillard Road, boomed along with it. This building at the corner of Whelpton Street and Drouillard Road was built in 1924 by Michael M Moodrey, a coal dealer, and originally housed a pharmacy. With its red brick, it is typical of many commercial buildings along Drouillard Road. By the late 1920s, it became home to the Crown Cafe. The Crown Cafe appears to have been a casualty of the Great Depression, closing in 1933.

In 1952, Ford announced it would be closing the Windsor assembly plant and moving the assembly operations and head office to Oakville. There were 4,300 jobs lost, many businesses suffered, and Drouillard Road began a slow decline through the next 30 years.

In 2019, the Grand Cantina restaurant opened on the main floor of the old Moodrey Building and became part of the revitalization of this stretch of Drouillard Road, which has recently seen a good deal of new investment and business openings.

ABOVE: **Assumption Church and College**, taken from the Ambassador Bridge tower under construction, circa 1929.

After closing its doors in 2014, **Assumption Church** began extensive renovations, welcoming back its parishioners in 2019. The church is surrounded by the University of Windsor—the secular descendant of **Assumption College**.

Assumption Church is one of the most beautiful churches in the city—the fourth home of the oldest continuously operating Roman Catholic parish west of Montreal. The majestic building at Riverside Drive and Huron Church Road was designed in the Gothic Revival style by Detroit architect Robert T Elliott. The first mass was held in the new church in 1845.

When this historic photograph was taken, this area on the edge of Sandwich Town was undergoing massive transformation. The Ambassador Bridge was being built, which would bring traffic, industry, and development in its wake. Soon to be dwarfed by the shadow of the bridge, Assumption Church and the Rosary Chapel—which was added in 1907—sit at centre, with the rectory visible just to the right. Behind the church, Assumption College was growing, too. The most recent addition was Dillon Hall, constructed in 1927, which sits at the far left.

Today, the Ambassador Bridge is the busiest international crossing between Canada and the United States. Assumption Church was one of the first sites in the city to be added to the heritage register in 1978. While shuttered for several years, the church building again serves the faithful and is undergoing a long-awaited architectural restoration. Assumption College is now the University of Windsor, and Dillon Hall is no longer on the fringes, but sits at the heart of campus.

This postcard from 1930 shows the newly opened **Ambassador Bridge**. Until the late 1990s, the bridge was painted a gloss jet-black.

In the early 20th century, the only way for passengers and goods to travel across the Detroit River was by boat or rail. After much debate, Canadian and American authorities approved a new international crossing, supported by American financier Joseph Bower, and built by the McClintic-Marshall Company—which later built the famous Golden Gate Bridge. Construction on what would become the Ambassador Bridge began in 1927. When it opened to ecstatic crowds in November 1929, the bridge welcomed vehicles (with an advertised three-and-a-half-minute commute) and pedestrians who could make the trip across the border on foot. For two years, the Ambassador Bridge was the largest suspension bridge in the world, only to be surpassed by the George Washington Bridge.

By the 1950s, millions of Americans crossed the bridge into Windsor, and bumper-to-bumper traffic became the norm. Today, the Ambassador Bridge remains one of the busiest international crossings in North America, with some 10,000 vehicles passing daily and one-quarter of Canadian-American trade each year. In recent decades, under the private ownership of the embattled Moroun family, the aging bridge has declined in upkeep. A new, publicly owned bridge, the Gordie Howe International Bridge, is in the works, to be built a few kilometres south of the Ambassador Bridge. As to the fate of the Ambassador Bridge, that remains to be seen.

Approaching 100 years in service, the **Ambassador Bridge** remains Windsor's most iconic landmark—though its future remains in question.

1940-1949

CHAPTER THREE

Industrial Powerhouse

The 1940s saw the rise of Windsor as a manufacturing powerhouse, as the city ramped up production to help with the needs of the British Empire and the Second World War. Local factories shifted production to make trucks, ambulances, and machine guns for the war effort. The population decline not only ended but the trend reversed as people flocked to the city to fill the jobs needed to support the war effort. The War Assets Corporation built a massive factory on Kildare Road in 1941 to assist with the demands of industrial production for the Second World War.

At the beginning of the 1940s, the population sat at 118,000, having remained stagnant for nearly a decade. The end of the decade saw the population rebound to 144,000 by 1949. As materials became available after the war, a need for housing was a priority. Luckily, Windsor had a surplus of vacant, serviced land. During the Great Depression, many tax defaults led to the City of Windsor becoming a major landholder of vacant property. It was easy to assemble large tracts of land for post-war housing developments. By the close of the war, more than 3,500 housing units had been built, with more to come in the years to follow. From the end of the Second World War to the mid 1950s, home building rose on a scale comparable to the prosperous years of the 1920s.

Organized labour also became a force during these years. The first United Auto Workers Local 195 was established in Windsor in December 1936. The UAW had organized Ford Canada by 1941, and a landmark 99-day strike and blockade at Ford in 1945 established the legitimacy of the union. The strike made membership mandatory for all non-management employees as well as established the payment of union dues by payroll deduction. By the end of the 1940s, there were approximately 30,000 union members in the ranks of the Windsor workforce and wages were among the highest paid in Canada.

During this period following the Great Depression, Windsor quickly re-established itself as an important manufacturing centre and rose to become the fourth-largest city in Canada in terms of gross value of manufactured products. From 1939 to 1953, industrial employment more than doubled from fewer than 20,000 employees to more than 43,000 as Windsor became an industrial powerhouse. Even in these boom years the desire to diversify by bringing in more varied industries was discussed, but manufacturing was king in a city built by labour.

Here, we take a look at industrial and commercial Windsor in the 1940s. Many of the scenes are only memories today, but they remain an important part of our industrial heritage, which is often overlooked.

• • •

TOP RIGHT: The original **Gray's** dry goods store sat at the corner of Ottawa Street and Gladstone Avenue.

Ottawa Street was a busy commercial district in the early 1940s, as seen here at the corner of Ottawa Street and Moy Avenue.

24

While **TD Bank** dominates the southeast corner at Moy today, mom-and-pop shops and local retailers are making a comeback along Ottawa Street.

This view from the early 1940s shows the southeast corner of Ottawa Street and Moy Avenue. A famous Windsor department store, Gray's, was located the other end of the block at Gladstone Avenue; you can spy a billboard for the department store sitting at the original location. The store had been founded by Harry Gray, a Jewish immigrant from Belarus, in 1929. Harry's son, Herb, would go on to be one of Windsor's most famous politicians, representing Windsor-West as its Member of Parliament from 1962 to 2002. In 1950, Gray's Department Store announced it had purchased the site on the corner of Moy Avenue, where it would erect a new store which it opened four years later. The new Gray's would be located in the building on the left-hand side on the southeast corner of where today's TD Bank now stands. The Gray family sold their interest in the business in 1962 to a group of businessmen from Toronto. In July 1986, Gray's Department Store announced it was going out of business and closed on January 26, 1989.

In 1882, Louis Greisinger Jr established British American Brewing Co. in a modest house facing the riverfront, peddling his signature offering: the Cincinnati Cream Lager. By 1896, the business had moved into this building, located on the same spot: the corner of Bruce Avenue and Sandwich Street (Riverside Drive West). In 1951, the brewery was merged with Bradings Capital Breweries from Ottawa and was renamed Bradings Breweries Ltd. In the last change of hands, Bradings was purchased by Carling Breweries, and the Windsor-based business was later renamed the Carling Brewery.

Carling Brewery was Windsor's oldest continuously operating brewery before it closed for good in 1969. The brewery was mostly demolished except for the newest part of the complex, which was a warehouse built in 1953.

British American Brewing Co. on Sandwich Street (Riverside Drive West), is seen here circa 1940.

In 1970, the site was purchased by the City of Windsor and two years later, planning was underway to convert the warehouse into the new Art Gallery of Windsor, which at the time, was housed in Willistead Manor. The gallery opened in the space in 1975. In 1994, the Art Gallery of Windsor moved out of the old brewery and into temporary quarters in Devonshire Mall, leasing the gallery building to the Ontario Casino Corporation. It became the temporary home of Casino Windsor until the permanent site opened in 1998. After surviving as a brewery, a gallery, and a casino, the warehouse was demolished.

The Art Gallery of Windsor was resurrected on the site in a modern structure of glass, stone, and metal. The new gallery opened in February 2001. Today, it shares the space with Museum Windsor, which occupies the first floor.

ABOVE: **The Art Gallery of Windsor** moved into this retrofitted warehouse in 1975.

With a design evoking a ship, the **Art Gallery of Windsor** opened in this purpose-built "architectural marvel" in 2001.

The ***Windsor Star*** with its iconic sign dominated the southwest corner of Ferry and Chatham streets, as seen here circa 1940.

Taking an existing apartment building on Ferry Street that was built in 1913, architect Albert McPhail worked that building into his design for the new Border Cities Star headquarters in 1927. The *Star* maintained their beaux-arts downtown office building for decades, adding a new printing press wing (with a state-of-the-art Crabtree Press) along Chatham Street in 1953.

The limestone arches are still a recognizable feature of the **University of Windsor's School of Social Work**.

The *Windsor Star* opened a new printing plant off EC Row Expressway in 1996, but the newsroom maintained its downtown presence. As time went on, however, the need for the large office building shrank. In 2012, it was announced that the *Windsor Star* would move their newsroom to the former Palace Cinema at Ouellette and University avenues. The University of Windsor announced plans to acquire the former news building, along with the former Armouries building downtown, and to convert them into academic buildings. CS&P Architects designed a plan that called for saving the facade of the *Star* building, with a new school campus building erected behind it. In 2016, the University of Windsor opened Windsor Hall, which houses its School of Social Work and Centre for Executive and Professional Education.

26

RIGHT: At Park and Pelissier streets, the **Norton Palmer Hotel** was a leading hotel in downtown Windsor in the 1940s.

Schoolchildren watch the **Norton Palmer** come down in 1975.

27

After the success of the Norton Hotel in downtown Detroit, owner Charles Norton turned his sights across the river. Partnering with Perry C Palmer, he opened the Norton-Palmer Hotel at the northwest corner of Park and Pelissier streets in December 1927. It was the tallest building in Windsor when it opened. Business boomed, and an expansion was made to the building in 1930, adding another 150 rooms to the hotel.

The hotel was run by Charles' son, Preston D Norton, until its closure in 1974. The building was sold to the Ontario Housing Corporation, which planned to demolish the hotel and replace it with a senior citizens' apartment building. The planned seniors complex fell through after the City of Windsor pulled out of the deal, feeling its share of the costs would be too high. The provincial government then put the site up for sale, and it was purchased by private developers in 1979. The 31-storey Victoria Park Place opened on the site in 1983, following its predecessor in holding the title of Windsor's tallest building until Caesars Windsor's Augustus Tower came along in 2008.

Victoria Park Place, a high-rise apartment building, occupies this prime spot today.

In 1941, to support the war effort, a large 337,000-square-foot factory was designed by the architectural firm of Allward & Gouinlock of Toronto. This $8-million factory was owned by the government's War Assets Corporation, but operated by Border Cities Industries, an arm's-length subsidiary of the General Motors (GM) Corporation of Canada. The factory building was constructed with amazing speed. The entire steel frame structure was erected in 21 days in the fall of 1941. The factory was built to produce high-speed Browning aircraft machine guns for the Second World War. The plant was fenced off from the rest of the General Motors complex, as the work for the war effort was guarded 24 hours a day. The factory aimed to offer employment to about 3,000 people, with at least 50 percent of them women. With the war underway, and a large number of men deployed overseas, the role of women was crucial to domestic production across North America for the war effort.

This plant at Kildare Road and Munsee Street was known as **Border Cities Industries** and produced machine guns during the Second World War.

Following the end of the war, the War Assets Corporation was charged with disposing of surplus assets. Being a fairly new, large factory, the Border Cities Industries building had numerous interested parties. In the end, the building was purchased in October 1946 by the Sandwich, Windsor & Amherstburg Railway as a new headquarters and garage for the transit company, replacing their previous location on University Avenue West. The garage was eventually purchased by General Motors Canada in 1978, and the then newly renamed Transit Windsor vacated the building and moved to their current garage and headquarters to Central Avenue and the EC Row Expressway in 1979. The old Border Cities Industries factory was incorporated into the renovation and expansion of the General Motors' existing transmission factory in 1981. The factory eventually closed, and the site was demolished and cleared between 2015 and 2017, leaving a gaping hole in Windsor's industrial landscape.

28

Once a giant in Windsor's automotive industry, this field is all that remains of the sprawling **General Motors** transmission plant.

Swimming in the Detroit River was a common pastime in the 1930s and 1940s, when public pools were few and far between. This municipal beach, originally known as the Ford City Bathing Beach, was located at George Avenue and Riverside Drive with a direct view of Belle Isle on the American side. It was built in 1928 on over an acreage of riverfront property, featuring a system of docks, diving boards, and a two-storey pavilion with changing rooms and a balcony at street level. It was a favourite spot of local teenagers, and district swimming championships were held here.

The park suffered from vandalism in the late 1950s, and a fire in 1957 damaged the dock and changing rooms, leading to the rebuilding and repair of the bathing beach structures. However, the glory days were quickly coming to an end. In late 1958, Dr John Howie, the medical officer of health to the Windsor Recreation Committee and the Windsor board of health, became concerned over the rising levels of pollution in the Detroit River. He had been raising the warning over the previous

The **East Windsor Bathing Beach** was a popular spot in the late 1940s.

18 years about the alarming increase of pollution in the water, and that year, his concern was raised to the point where he nearly ordered the beach closed. Over the winter, water quality continued to decline, and in April 1959, he recommended that the beach be permanently closed.

In May 1959, the idea to permanently close the East Windsor Bathing Beach came before City Council. Everyone had become resigned to the fact that pollution levels made swimming in the Detroit River impractical, and the motion passed without debate. The structures were demolished and removed from the site shortly after. The City of Windsor acquired the property immediately to the west of the East Windsor Bathing Beach and opened Alexander Park, which was dedicated in 1959 in honour of Viscount Alexander of Tunis, who was Canada's Governor General at the time. In August 1961, the former East Windsor Bathing Beach lands were officially incorporated into Alexander Park.

Today, **Alexander Park** sits at the foot of George Avenue at Riverside Drive.

29

An aerial view of Windsor's riverfront, between Goyeau Street and Ouellette Avenue, circa 1940s.

For much of its early life, Windsor boasted a working riverfront—the beating heart of an industrial city. Along the strait, by the downtown core, was a network of rail lines, train and car ferries, and a range of businesses and taverns. In particular, the Windsor-Detroit Ferry Company docks at the end of Ouellette Avenue were a mainstay of downtown, allowing cars and passengers to cross back and forth between Windsor and Detroit. After the Detroit-Windsor Tunnel and the Ambassador Bridge connected the two cities, the popularity of passenger boats declined until ferry service ended in 1938. To the east, by Goyeau Avenue, the Canadian National Railway station is also visible. It closed in 1961.

In the mid-1950s, the City of Windsor embarked on a mission to transform the riverfront. In 1953, they expropriated the Windsor-Detroit Ferry Company docks and slated the area for demolition the following year. A new retaining wall was built—the first step to creating Dieppe Gardens, which opened in 1959. Over the years to come, the expulsion of business and retail from the riverfront would continue, championed by the likes of Mayor Bert Weeks. Large hotels came down, and railway tracks were pulled up. Nearly continuous riverfront parkland would be developed from the Ambassador Bridge down to Hiram Walker & Sons Distillery, including numerous parks connected by a trail, which opened in 1999 and remains today.

30

Windsor's riverfront has undergone a decades-long transformation into a downtown park, boasting walking trails, manicured landscaping, and a sculpture garden.

1950-1975

CHAPTER FOUR

A Very Modern City

At mid-century, Windsor was a city on the verge of renewal. New building projects were set to modernize the look and feel of downtown. Development continued around the fringes, expanding to the west, south, and east, but leaving the older parts of the city neglected and lacking in investment. In 1966, amalgamation added the former Town of Riverside, portions of the townships of Sandwich East, Sandwich South, and Sandwich West, as well as the former Town of Ojibway to the City of Windsor.

The 1950s and 1960s saw massive investment into the core part of the city with plans for urban renewal. The civic centre was completely rebuilt: the Municipal Courthouse opened on City Hall Square on 1957, followed by a new City Hall in 1959. The Essex County Courthouse relocated from Mackenzie Hall in Sandwich to the new downtown court building opposite City Hall in 1963. The new Ontario Tourist Centre opened in 1963 at Goyeau and Park streets. A major department store, apartment building, and parking garage were all built in the area around the same time.

On the west side of Ouellette Avenue, investment was happening as well. All of the buildings on the north side of Riverside Drive were demolished and Dieppe Park was established. The rehabilitation of the François Baby House into what was then the Hiram Walker Historical Museum occurred in 1958, and the Cleary Auditorium and Memorial Convention Hall anchored the renewal on the west side of downtown. In 1973, the Windsor Public Library moved out of the Carnegie Library that had been its home for 70 years and into what was then a state-of-the-art modern library on Ouellette Avenue just south of Elliott Street. This was a period of civic building unrivalled in the city's history.

It was also a period of turmoil and uncertainty when, in 1954, Ford of Canada closed its assembly operations and relocated the head office and factory to Oakville. This culminated in large job losses with significant economic repercussions on the surrounding neighbourhood that would continue to be felt long after the factory was demolished.

Windsor as most of us know and remember it took shape during this period. The city pushed forward, embracing an idea of progress where new replaced old and old was modernized. Windsor never held a great appreciation for the past. Preservation of historic structures was never a priority, and the prevailing opinion of what constituted an historic property was also debated. Most of the buildings that we see today in old photographs, and lament their loss, were generally only 50 to 70 years old when they were demolished. It's the perfect time period where a building is old, but not quite old enough to raise an outcry.

This trend and cycle repeats to this day, most recently with the new City Hall replacing the previous one after a little over 60 years. In particular, the downtown Windsor we know today was born in this post-war push for progress. Many of the remains of Victorian Windsor met the wrecking ball, with Dieppe Park being born, and other civic projects. New libraries, banks, and office buildings replaced older ones, and for the most part, few tears were shed.

• • •

This photograph from the early 1950s shows the northwest corner of Ouellette Avenue and Riverside Drive West. At the time, the building was home to its final tenant, the Ritz Hotel. The building, known as the Medbury Block, opened in 1883 as the home to the Merchant's Bank of Canada. It was a grand imposing structure designed by Detroit architects Donaldson & Meier in the Second Empire style of architecture. The building's large tower was a landmark on the north side of Riverside Drive—but it

The **Ritz Hotel** had a prime riverfront location at the end of Ouellette Avenue, circa 1950.

The **Cleary Guest House** was built at the bequest of Edmund Cleary in 1957.

found itself in the way of a planned city waterfront park. In 1954, the owner agreed to sell the property to the City of Windsor, and the building was demolished in 1955. While work continued on the riverfront's transformation for decades, Dieppe Gardens was dedicated in 1959.

The Cleary Guest House, nestled down close to the water, was made possible by a bequest to the City that was laid out in the will of Edmund Anderson Cleary. Edmund was a lawyer in Windsor for more than 50 years, and was the son of former Mayor Francis Cleary. The younger Cleary left $500,000 (adjusted for inflation, equivalent to about $4 million today) when he died in 1955, with specific instructions to build a Civic Auditorium to bear his name. Included in the donation, he earmarked $20,000 to be put towards a Guest House at the new park. Even the layout and design of the building was laid out clearly: the will instructed that it must be two storeys, with restrooms and a concession on the main floor. The second floor was to be open on two sides—one facing the city, one facing the river. The message "WELCOME" was to be put on both the east and west ends of the building. After 50 years of service, the much (unfairly) maligned Guest House, with its distinctive mid-century modern design, was demolished during the summer of 2007 and replaced with the Riverfront Peace Beacon, a multi-purpose building that hosts a restaurant and patio, which remains today.

The **Peace Beacon**, with a waterfront bistro, is the only downtown retailer that sits north of Riverside Drive, nestled into Dieppe Gardens.

The **François Baby House** was being renovated as Windsor's first museum in 1956.

Originally built in 1812 by François Baby, a member of one of Windsor's founding families, construction was stopped when the house was seized by General William Hull of the United States Army and used as the American headquarters for the invasion of Upper Canada. The home—which was commonly known as Le Ferme—went through many uses and changes throughout the years, being split into a duplex around 1890. The house ended up abandoned in the 1930s during the Great Depression.

In June 1940, plans were launched to restore the property and turn the building over to the City of Windsor to operate as a museum. When originally built, the front of the house was on the north side and faced the river. The building was recognized by the Historic Sites and Monuments Board of Canada as a National Historic Site in 1950. The building was largely rebuilt to give the historic appearance that's seen today. In 1956, Hiram Walker & Sons Limited stepped in with the cash needed to finish the renovations, and two years later, the Hiram Walker Historical Museum opened its doors to the public. Today, the house is part of Museum Windsor and houses permanent galleries on Windsor's French heritage, the War of 1812, the Battle of Windsor, and the history of the residence itself.

Today, the **Maison François Baby House** is part of Museum Windsor.

32

This building survived many different lives. It was originally built around 1870 as the home of Vital Ouellette—the man who lent his name to Windsor's main street. The house used to sit on the corner of Chatham Street East and Ouellette Avenue. After Vital Ouellette passed away, the family rented out the home until it was sold to Cameron & Curry around 1887. In 1899, the lot on the corner was sold to the Bank of Montreal to build a bank branch, and the building was moved over one lot to its present site. It was the first brick building moved in Windsor. Interestingly, the building was just shifted east, and not rotated, leaving what was originally the front facade facing the alley and the back of the bank.

ABOVE: This vintage brochure for the **Windsor Castle Cafe** dates back to about 1935.

The **Commodore Supper Club** was a popular spot in mid-century Windsor.

The residence was then split into in a duplex and rented out until it was leased by the Windsor Club in 1903 as a clubhouse for $500 a year. The Windsor Club lasted from March 1904 until 1929, when the club nearly went bankrupt and had to sell off the building. After going through a few other tenants, the Commodore Supper Club was opened in 1936 by Joseph Gan. The Commodore closed after a fire in 1979 and reopened as Jason's. It has rotated through a variety of adult entertainment venues or restaurants. This building shows how uses can evolve. What was built as a residence was only used for that purpose for about three decades, while for the last 120 years, it has served downtown as an entertainment club.

33

This spot on Chatham Street East has been home to many Windsor entertainment venues.

Down the alley behind the Bank of Montreal, the original facade of **Vital Ouellette**'s house can be spotted—a hint to the building's past.

ABOVE: **Windsor's Carnegie Library**, at the corner of Victoria Avenue and Park Street West, in 1953.

Boasting an in-vogue brutalist style, a new main library branch opened on Ouellette Avenue to much fanfare in 1973.

At the turn of the 20th century, the city's existing library at Ferry and Chatham streets had become far too inadequate for the needs of the growing city, and the library board set out to replace it. John Scott & Co. of Detroit drew up the plans, and a request was made to American philanthropist Andrew Carnegie. Carnegie made his fortune in steel and by the late 19th century, he was one of the richest Americans in history. During the last 18 years of his life, from 1901 to 1919, he gave away roughly $350 million dollars (equivalent to more than $5 billion today). One of his major bequests were for building

34

The name, **Carnegie Apartments**, is the only clue to this location's literary past.

community public libraries. His donations helped to build 2,509 public libraries around the world, including 125 in Canada. The Windsor Library board made a request to Carnegie, and on February 13, 1901, Windsor was granted $20,000 dollars—the first location in Canada to be awarded a library grant. As construction got underway, it quickly became evident that the original allotment was not going to be sufficient for the project, and Carnegie gave an additional $7,000 dollars.

While Windsor received the first Carnegie grant, disputes over location and delays in construction prevented it from being the first one in Canada to open, with that honour going to Chatham. The Windsor Carnegie Library opened to the public on October 16, 1903, from the corner of Victoria Avenue and Park Street West in the downtown core. Within a few decades, however, complaints began that the library was too cramped to accommodate demand, and a large addition was built to house a children's library. By the late 1960s, plans began for a new main library branch. The highly modern replacement, Central Library—with its brutalist architectural style the antithesis of the old Carnegie library—opened its doors in 1973 at 850 Ouellette Avenue. The Carnegie Library closed November 14, 1973, and was reduced to rubble shortly after. Today, an apartment building is on the site of the former library at Victoria Avenue and Park Street West.

This view from the late 1960s looks west from the top of the staircase at Our Lady of the Rosary Church at Riverside Drive East and Drouillard Road. Ford Plant One is visible closest to the church, while the Hiram Walker & Sons Limited distillery can be seen in the far distance. At the time this photograph was taken, Ford Plant One and the offices along both the north and south sides of Riverside Drive were mostly empty and unused since Ford Canada had transferred its assembly operations and head office from Windsor to Oakville in 1953. Ford Plant One was built between 1910 and 1916 to supplement the original Walkerville Wagon Works, which was the birthplace of Ford Canada. This is where the infamous Ford Strike of 1945 occurred (which lasted 99 days) and while it resulted in major gains for union recognition, it is commonly believed to be the reason that Ford Canada abandoned its Windsor operation.

As seen here in the 1960s, **Ford Plant One** and **Holy Rosary Church** sat at the end of Drouillard Road, forming the heart of old Ford City.

While the church building still stands, the riverfront land where **Ford Plant One** stood has been empty for decades.

By 1969, the old factory met the wrecking ball, and the large complex that covered 17 acres was left empty. Ford Plant One, which stood for just over 50 years, has now been gone as long as it was standing. Ford City, the neighbourhood surrounding the factory and an independent municipality until 1935, suffered greatly with the Ford Canada move to Oakville, setting off an economic depression in the area that would last for decades.

Our Lady of the Rosary Roman Catholic Church survived Ford City's decline, but stopped serving the area as a church in 2007. It has been revitalized as a privately owned events venue.

35

The **Maple Leaf Hotel** on a then-industrial stretch of Howard Avenue in 1960.

Built on Howard Avenue, just south of Hanna Street East during the boom years of the 1920s, the Howard Block was like many buildings built around the city at that time: three storefronts on the ground floor with apartments above. The building was built in the middle of a mostly residential block and may seem out of place today, but the opposite side of Howard Avenue at the time was industrial in nature, with the Champion Spark Plug factory across the street. The building fell vacant during the Depression and became City of Windsor property for unpaid taxes in 1934. It was recommended by the building inspector to be converted into a fire hall or a garage and workshop for city vehicles. The building was eight years old when it became City property and had been completely looted and stripped. Many buildings and vacant lots were abandoned during the height of the Great Depression and defaulted to City ownership for unpaid taxes. Nothing ever happened with the building inspector's suggestion for this building and the City ended up leasing it to a business with an option to buy in 1935. The option was exercised in 1936. The Maple Leaf Hotel opened in the building around 1937 and ran through 1964. By 2014, the building had again fallen vacant and became boarded up, but remained largely in its original condition. In 2016, the building was cleaned up, reclad, and the original architectural elements covered over—its humble past a secret.

The doorframes on this apartment complex are the only hint that this building on Howard Avenue may be older than it appears.

36

This view looks east down Windsor Avenue towards Wyandotte Street East in 1960.

Windsor Outboard Motors sat on the southeast corner of Windsor Avenue and Wyandotte Street East in 1960. Despite the name, the business dealt in all kinds of goods. They sold bicycles, skis, skates, and toys. Across the street, on the northeast corner, is a former service station that was then home to Veteran Cab. Veteran Cab is so named as it was started by fourteen veterans who used their war service gratuities and re-establishment credits to purchase six new cars to start the company in the fall of 1945. Veteran Cab remains active today and has its current office one block south of its original location.

Windsor Arena dominates the left side of the photograph. The arena was designed by engineers AW Connor & Co. and opened in 1925 as Border Cities Arena. From 1926 to 1927, the Detroit Cougars Hockey Team played their first season in Windsor's arena as the Olympia in Detroit was still under construction. The Cougars were renamed the Red Wings in 1932. The arena too was rebranded as Windsor Arena, but locals knew it better as the Barn. It was the home of teams such as the Bulldogs and the Spitfires. The Spitfires played their last game on December 4, 2008, but the arena remained in use until 2013. Today, however, the Barn sits empty and its future remains uncertain.

The **Windsor Arena**, better known as the Barn, sits empty on a now-quiet stretch of Windsor Avenue.

This photograph, which appears at first to be a rural scene in Essex County, is actually a view looking south from the intersection of Walker Road and Ypres Avenue taken in August 1950. On the right side of the photo is the Bigness Inn and Service Station. Run by South Walkerville resident JF Bigness, he first opened his service station in 1926 and ran it until his passing in 1964. Note the grassy median on Walker Road as well as the fields of crops that are the location of the Windsor Assembly Plant today. The massive assembly plant was founded by Chrysler of Canada in 1928 and underwent many expansions over the years before a complete retooling to make minivans in 1983. Today, the Windsor Assembly is the last remaining assembly plant of the Big Three automotive companies left in Canada's original Motor City.

Walker Road is surrounded by empty fields in 1950.

Today, Walker Road is dwarfed by **FCA Canada's Windsor Assembly Plant**.

38

Here is a view looking east from the west side of the intersection of Giles Boulevard West and Ouellette Avenue in March 1952.

In the 1950s, the Essex County War Memorial was located in the middle of Giles Boulevard. The memorial, which was originally created to honour the fallen of the First World War, was built of Canadian pink granite and designed by local architect George Y Masson and dedicated on November 11, 1924. It was built at a cost of $25,000 dollars and funded by donations from local citizens. In 1932, a large house was demolished on the northeast corner of Ouellette Avenue and Giles Boulevard East and replaced with a gas station. The transformation of the area into a more commercial zone prompted

LEFT: The **Essex County War Memorial** honours Windsor's fallen from City Hall Square.

RIGHT: While the cenotaph has moved, a **Rexall** drugstore still occupies this corner of Giles Boulevard West and Ouellette Avenue.

consideration to move the cenotaph from what was becoming a busy intersection to a more serene location. Plans were proposed to move the monument to Jackson Park, but with the Great Depression in full swing the money was not available for such a project and the monument would remain in place for another 30 years. The monument was eventually relocated in April 1965. The 106-ton monument was dismantled, stone by stone, cleaned, and rebuilt at City Hall Square where it remains today.

In the post-war years, downtown Windsor was the place to be, as seen here at the intersection of Wyandotte Street and Ouellette Avenue in October 1950.

The hustle and bustle of the main intersection of downtown Windsor is evident in this photo from October 1950. What this view reveals, however, is the contrast between old and new Windsor. Large old houses dominate the streetscape; even in the 1950s, this intersection was far more residential than commercial. On the northeast corner is a Pond's Drug Store. Pond's was a local Windsor business started by WA Pond in 1899, and eventually grew to eight branches across the city. The Pond's chain was incorporated in 1928 and put up for sale and purchased by Big V Pharmacies Ltd. The store relocated to Park Street West and Ouellette Avenue in 1966, and the store shown above was closed. In 1995, Big V was sold to Shoppers Drug Mart Inc. The view of the intersection today shows that many changes have occurred in the last 70 years—it is hard to believe that downtown's main intersection was once largely residential.

Homes are nowhere in sight, but downtown Windsor is quieter today than in decades past.

The Ottawa Street business district rivalled downtown's offerings in the 1950s and 1960s. Seen here in the summer of 1960, the second location of Tepperman's—the building on the corner of Ottawa Street and Pierre Avenue—opened its doors in 1940. The furniture business was so successful that they added a second and third floor in 1947. Eventually, they outgrew the building and moved out of Ottawa Street in 1978 to their present home on Ouellette Avenue. The large building did not remain empty long and was purchased by UAW Local 195 for use as a union hall in 1979. UAW Local 195 was the first UAW local in Canada, having been founded in 1936 when employees from Kelsey Wheel joined the union. Today, it is a multi-purpose office.

The Ottawa Street business district, looking east from Pierre Avenue, in June 1960.

Across the street from Tepperman's in 1960 is Kingdom Hall. Built as a neighbourhood theatre around 1923, it opened as the Regent Theatre. In 1946, after the war, the theatre was completely gutted and rebuilt. It reopened that same year as the Kent Theatre with 478 seats. At the time, however, small neighbourhood theatres began to see declining attendance as television ownership rose, and the Kent closed in 1957. Soon after, it reopened once again, this time by local Jehovah's Witnesses as a Kingdom Hall and remained as such through the late 1980s. Today, while much has changed, the important things remain: Ottawa Street is a still mainstay for local businesses.

While many of the businesses have come and gone, most of the buildings on this stretch of Ottawa Street are still standing 60 years later.

41

What would become the town of Riverside seceded from Sandwich East Township in 1921, and narrowly dodged annexation by the City of Windsor in 1935. It was a French settler community, many working their ribbon farms well into the 20th century. Under the guidance of its first mayor, William St. Louis, the community grew in size to 5000 people by 1930, with new streets and development apace. At its heart, however, Riverside remained a small, tight-knit community. According to local historian Patrick Brode, residents remember swimming in the river, riding the tides, and that Riverside Drive, even into the 1940s, only boasted a few large houses with wide swatches of land in between.

ABOVE: In the 1950s, the shores of the Detroit River in the town of **Riverside** were largely cottage country.

In the shadow of the **Riverside Brewery**, these nine houses were deemed uninhabitable by the Board of Health in 1952 and slated for demolition.

Today, this stretch of Riverside Drive is home to **Sandpoint Beach**. Long gone are the cottages and docked boats. This area is now called **Millionaire's Row**, boasting the city's most prized real estate.

The Riverside Brewery set up in the middle of this humble waterfront community, surrounded by cottages, in 1923. It was designed to take advantage of Prohibition, brewing beer for direct export to the United States. After Prohibition ended, however, the company was bought up by Canadian Breweries and shuttered by 1935. It gained new life in 1941 as a storage and sorting facility for Essex Hybrid Seed Company, but was vacant by 1965. After over 50 years sitting neglected, the Riverside Brewery met the wrecking ball in 2018.

Cottage country is also a thing of the past. Grand homes are squeezed along Riverside Drive—the most coveted postal code in the city. Sandpoint Beach is the only vestige of what once was, and its five acres constitute Windsor's most popular public beach.

42

One of the things that Windsor is most famous for is not about the city at all—rather, it is about the neighbour across the river. For many, one of the best things that our city has to offer is its view of the Detroit skyline.

Detroit, however, has played a much more important role in Windsor's history. Our earliest settlers were connected to Fort Detroit. A war was fought—and some suggest won—across this river. Self-emancipated Black men, women, and children escaped slavery across the Detroit River during the years of the Underground Railroad, establishing a community in the heart of Windsor. The auto industry jumped across the strait, first with Ford of Canada, turning Windsor into a mini-Motor City. Emancipation Day brought families from Detroit and Windsor back together, bringing luminaries and musicians from afar to celebrate Black heritage and accomplishments. The International

A view of the **Detroit** skyline looking north from Windsor's downtown, circa 1954.

Not only has Windsor's downtown transformed, but Detroit's has, too: today, their cityscape is dominated by the **Renaissance Center** (which opened in 1976) and the **TCF Center** (formerly Cobo Hall and Cobo Center), which opened in 1960.

Freedom Festival—with its trademark fireworks over the Detroit River—celebrate this historic bond between the two cities.

Today, some might argue that our skyline and obsession with progress led us to try to mimic the skyscrapers of Detroit, or that our riverfront parks serve to gaze upon our metropolis neighbour. We Windsorites, however, don't seem to mind—proudly calling ourselves South Detroit every chance we get.

WINDSOR
ONTARIO, CANADA

Rise of the Border Cities
1800s–1919

1. Essex County Courthouse / Mackenzie Hall Cultural Centre
2. Sandwich Street
3. Dougall Avenue Public School
4. First Presbyterian Church / All Nations Full Gospel Church
5. Norwich Block / One Riverside Drive
6. Hôtel-Dieu Hospital / Windsor Regional Hospital
7. Shores Acres Hotel / Ernest Atkinson Park
8. Labelle Building
9. Hiram Walker & Sons Limited
10. Windsor Jockey Club / Jackson Park

Roaring Twenties & Dirty Thirties
1920–1939

11. WD Lowe / Giles Campus French Immersion Public School
12. Imperial Bank of Canada / Walkerville
13. SW&A Car Barns
14. St. Mary's Academy / The Gates of St. Mary Subdivision
15. Windsor Collegiate Institute / Food Basics Parking Lot
16. Wyandotte Street, east from Ouellette Avenue
17. City Hall
18. Post Office / Paul Martin Building
19. Devonshire Race Track / Devonshire Mall
20. Drouillard-Wyandotte Underpass
21. 1000 Drouillard Road
22. Assumption Church
23. Ambassador Bridge

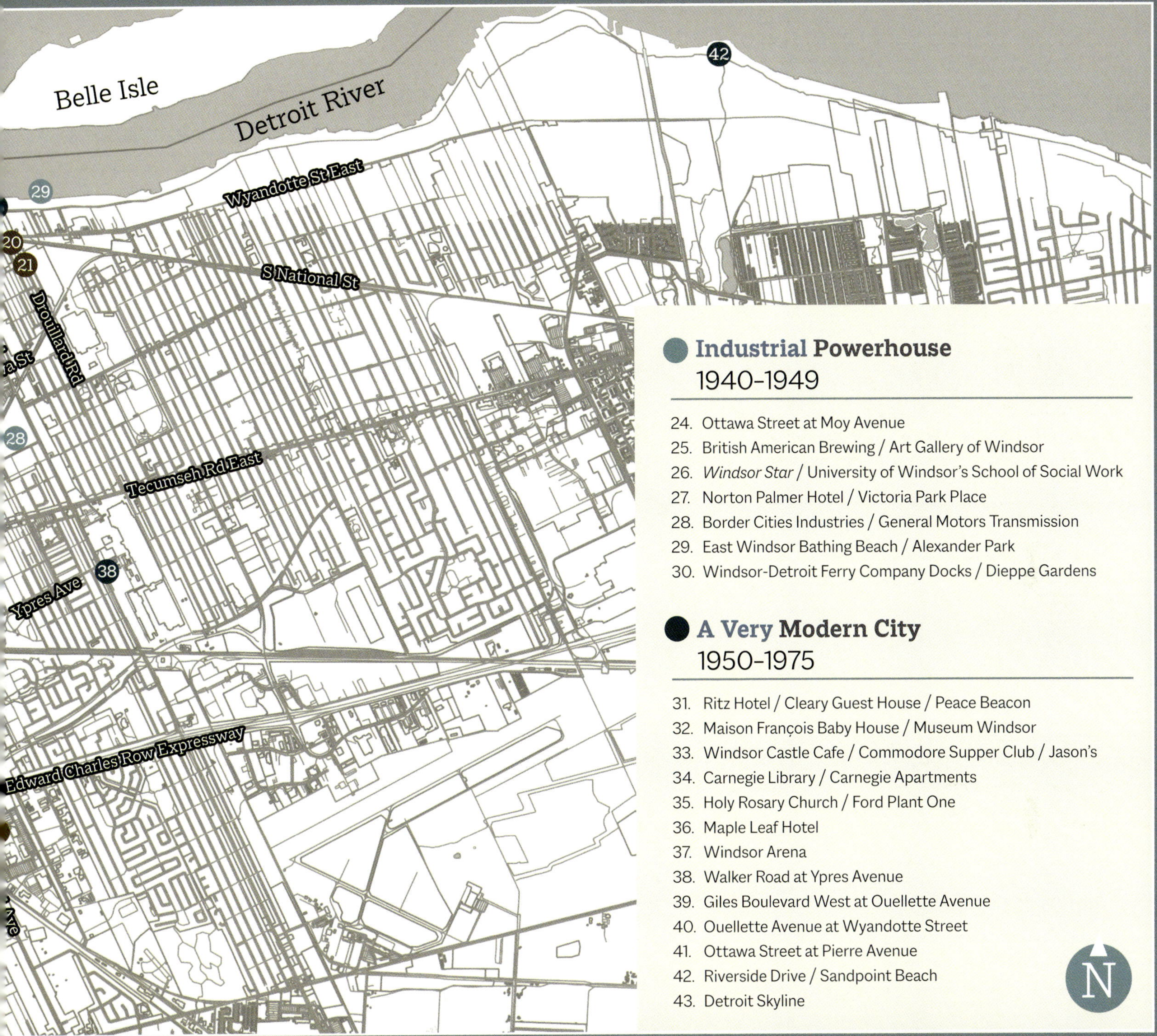

Industrial Powerhouse
1940–1949

24. Ottawa Street at Moy Avenue
25. British American Brewing / Art Gallery of Windsor
26. *Windsor Star* / University of Windsor's School of Social Work
27. Norton Palmer Hotel / Victoria Park Place
28. Border Cities Industries / General Motors Transmission
29. East Windsor Bathing Beach / Alexander Park
30. Windsor-Detroit Ferry Company Docks / Dieppe Gardens

A Very Modern City
1950–1975

31. Ritz Hotel / Cleary Guest House / Peace Beacon
32. Maison François Baby House / Museum Windsor
33. Windsor Castle Cafe / Commodore Supper Club / Jason's
34. Carnegie Library / Carnegie Apartments
35. Holy Rosary Church / Ford Plant One
36. Maple Leaf Hotel
37. Windsor Arena
38. Walker Road at Ypres Avenue
39. Giles Boulevard West at Ouellette Avenue
40. Ouellette Avenue at Wyandotte Street
41. Ottawa Street at Pierre Avenue
42. Riverside Drive / Sandpoint Beach
43. Detroit Skyline

N

Acknowledgements

It's certainly no easy task to sit down and think about offering thanks to all the people who've played a part directly and indirectly in the book you are now holding in your hands. I have to start by thanking my wife, Natasha. Her help as my first set of eyes reviewing and reading and offering her input was invaluable as I worked on this project. There were many evenings where I retreated to the office to write, and her support helped immensely and was greatly appreciated. I also must thank my parents, John and Janice, for instilling in me a sense of the importance of the past. Many childhood trips to museums and many grand homes around England left a mark on me and helped me forge a love of architecture and appreciation of history from an early age. I must also give thanks to my editor, Sharon, who helped keep this project on track and focused. To all the readers of the website internationalmetropolis.com over the years—thank you. It seems that there is now an appreciation and a desire to protect the past locally that we haven't seen in a long time. Also, a big thank you to everyone involved with history and heritage whose paths have crossed mine over the years on both sides of the river.

Andrew Foot

• • •

Working on this book has been the opportunity of a lifetime. I would like to thank my grandfather, Bob Grondin, for opening my eyes to the rich history of our city through our afternoon drives. My editor to the stars, Sharon Hanna, for believing in my work and providing me with constant guidance and reassurance. Without you none of this would have been possible. I would also like to thank my fiancée. Katie Pfaff makes me feel like anything is possible with every breath she takes. Her unbeatable drive forward pushes me to be a better person every day. Lastly, I would like to thank my father, Nevin Virtue. Without him I would never have picked up a camera. Watching him capture priceless moments throughout my childhood is the reason I began my career as a photographer. For that, I am forever grateful.

Ian Virtue

Biographies

ANDREW FOOT is Windsor's leading architectural historian. He has documented the built history of Windsor and Essex County online for the past two decades. Andrew exhibited twice at the Art Gallery of Windsor, and published a companion guidebook to one of the exhibitions entitled *Windsor Modern*. Andrew has been actively involved in the preservation of Windsor's heritage since 2004 as a volunteer member of the former Windsor Heritage Committee and currently as a member of the Heritage Standing Committee. His research on local architectural history can be found online at internationalmetropolis.com. He enjoys travelling and taking in architecture and culture around the world. Andrew lives with his wife in Windsor.

• • •

IAN VIRTUE is a landscape and commercial photographer based in Essex County. He and his camera have travelled the world, capturing the mountains of Nepal, the rolling wildness of Canada's west, the beaches of Thailand, and more. You can find his photographic rediscovery of his hometown during the COVID-19 pandemic at ianvirtue.com/the-windsor-project. Ian also works with Arctic Basecamp, a climate advocacy organization focused on speaking science to power. When Ian isn't out taking photos he can be found in the kitchen making home-cooked meals, hiking, or enjoying a glass of wine on Pelee Island with his fiancée Katie.

DOUGALL
PARK